*To Pat and Hans,
Hope you enjoy
the memories —
Sandy*

Memories of Crystal Beach Park, Vermilion, Ohio

Sandra Calvert Mueller

Memories of Crystal Beach Park, Vermilion, Ohio

Sandra Calvert Mueller
Marlene Calvert Feldkamp
Tom Ryan

Memories of Crystal Beach Park, Vermilion, Ohio

Copyright © 2007 Sandra Calvert Mueller, Marlene Calvert Feldkamp, and Tom Ryan. All rights reserved. No part of this book may be reproduced or retransmitted in any form or by any means without the written permission of the publisher.

Published by Wheatmark™
610 East Delano Street, Suite 104
Tucson, Arizona 85705 U.S.A.
www.wheatmark.com

Publisher's Cataloging-In-Publication Data
(Prepared by The Donohue Group, Inc.)

Mueller, Sandra Calvert.
Memories of Crystal Beach Park, Vermilion, Ohio / Sandra Calvert Mueller, Marlene Calvert Feldkamp, and Tom Ryan.

p. : ill. ; cm.

ISBN: 978-1-58736-852-3 (hardcover)
ISBN: 978-1-58736-851-6 (pbk.)

1. Crystal Beach Park (Vermilion, Ohio)—History. 2. Amusement parks—Ohio—Vermilion—History. I. Feldkamp, Marlene Calvert. II. Ryan, Tom (Tom Patrick), 1938– III. Title.

GV1853.3.O3 C79 2007
791.068/77122   2007926359

Contents

Acknowledgments xi
Preface xiii
Introduction 1
The Founding Family 3
The Early Years 9
The Golden Years 36
After the Fire 83
Picnics and Other Attractions 96
The Sunset Years 103
Epilogue 110

This book is dedicated to our grandparents George and Josephine Blanchat, who started it all;

To our parents, Thelma and Jim Calvert and Eleanor and Jimmy Ryan, who helped to ensure the legacy of memories by taking photos and organizing information over the years;

And to all those who loved the park as much as we did…this is for you.

A Memory

Somewhere along the Erie Shore
A ballroom stands from days of yore.
Shattered by the storm and rain,
Only fond memories will remain.

The people came from miles around,
To dance and listen to the sound
Of music from the greatest bands,
That stopped to make their one night stands.

Lombardo, Dorsey, Brown and Kaye,
Were just a few who passed this way,
To leave behind the haunting strain
Of many lovely old refrains
That fill the air and still can reach
All those who remember Crystal Beach.

Eleanor Blanchat Ryan
1990

Acknowledgments

We are most grateful for the encouragement and support of our families in our endeavor to share memories of Crystal Beach Park. Thank you, David, Carole, Michael, Katie, Sara, Mike, Peter, Janet, Colleen, Jack, Tom, and Michele for being there for us.

Special thanks go to family members who directly participated in helping to get the project started, supplying valuable photos, and lending their artistic ability to this book. Your help, Tara, Todd, Cathy, Chris, and Susanne, was very important in the formation of the final product.

Thank you to Albert Doane and Pat Smith, who were other sources of valuable pictures and information.

A particular mention should be made in recognition of George Murphy. His generosity in contributing to this book resulted in our being able to feature many more photos of individuals who had lived and worked at the park. With his passing in 2006, we lost a good friend.

We regret if we have omitted anyone's name from the book who had participated at the park. Please know that any omission was unintentional.

Preface

The nice thing about memories is, once you've made them, they aren't easily taken away.

They may be pushed way back into a far corner of the mind, left to gather dust, and seemingly forgotten. Then someone brings out the photo album, and it's like a floodgate opens up to wash away all the dust. The memories are now as clear as if they happened yesterday…not decades ago.

We've decided to bring out our photo album to help bring back for some of you memories of your youth. For others it is our way of sharing with you a very special time and place that you may have only heard about…or perhaps never knew existed.

We hope you enjoy your journey.

Introduction

In its early history, the forty-two and a half acres that was to become Crystal Beach Park was owned by George W. Shadduck. Shadduck purchased the property on November 10, 1854, for $1,275 at public sale. A judgement and order of sale against a Richard S. Harris by a Giles Williams resulted in the sale. Frederick W. Cogswell, master commissioner of Erie County, was in charge of the sale that was held at the Court of Common Pleas in Sandusky. In the 1854 deed, the forty-two and a half acres was referred to as "being the same purchased by George Hubbard of Horace Thompson." The land was located on the north end of lot 27 in the first section of Vermilion township in Erie County, Ohio.

A land option document between the Shadduck heirs and George Blanchat, recorded August 28, 1906, further described the Shadduck property as being bordered on the north by Lake Erie, and on the east by the Erie and Lorain County line. At that time, the Shadduck property was bordered on the south by land owned by Mrs. L. M. (Alice) Todd. The western side of Shadduck's property was bordered by land owned by George Lohr. George Lohr's land is now known as Nakomis Park.

The house on the property had been a stagecoach stop and a popular stopping off place for wayside travelers since the early 1870s. There was a cupola, which, before being removed, was reported to have been used as a lookout tower against Indian attacks.

As travelers continued to stop for lunch and enjoy the lake that bordered Mr. Shadduck's farm, he decided to allow them to drive their buggies down to the beach. This led to the transforming of his twenty-two and a half acres of lakeside property, around 1874, into a picnic grove complete with beer garden and dance hall. With the added attraction of a roulette wheel, the grove soon became known as Little Monte Carlo. Vermilion resident George "Pete" Wahl ran a tent carousel, which was added around 1898 to what was now known as

Shadduck's Grove. Wahl also owned and operated a shooting gallery on the property.

In 1906 a successful Lorain businessman named George H. Blanchat heard of Shadduck's death and that his heirs, George W. and Vera Shadduck, Frank G. Lynn, Eva May Lynn Scholl and husband Charles Scholl, and Leana Shadduck, wished to sell Shadduck's Grove.

Blanchat had previously owned the Star Theater, Railway Depot, and a bar and grill at the corner of Broadway and Lake Road in Lorain, Ohio. This bar and grill was located where Heilman's Restaurant was later built. Blanchat was then the owner and operator of a scenic picnic and boat area at Oak Point, located four miles west of Lorain. This area is now called Beaver Park. These business experiences encouraged Blanchat's vision for the Shadduck property. He was aware that Cedar Point was the only amusement park between Cleveland and Toledo and believed that the acquisition of Shadduck's Grove would be a golden opportunity to establish another amusement park to serve the community.

On October 27, 1906, Blanchat purchased Shadduck's Grove for fourteen thousand dollars and moved his wife, Josephine, and one-and-a-half-year-old daughter, Thelma, to Vermilion. They lived in the stagecoach house until their new home was built next door in 1907.

Blanchat added rides, concessions, and attractions to what some people referred to as the "park of a thousand trees." Shelter could be built for fifteen thousand picnickers. There was ample room on the property for parking five thousand vehicles.

Under new management, a new name was needed. One day, while Josephine and George were walking along the beach, Josephine picked up some sand and let the sparkling grains sift through her fingers. With her remark, "It looks like crystal," Crystal Beach Park was born.

On Decoration Day (now referred to as Memorial Day), Thursday, May 30, 1907, Crystal Beach Park opened for its first of fifty-five seasons.

The Founding Family

George Blanchat, our grandfather, was the founder of Crystal Beach Park.

Josephine Blanchat, our grandmother, shared equally in the family-owned business. These photos were taken around 1900.

The Blanchat daughters, Thelma and Eleanor, are seen here in the late 1920s. They assumed ownership of Crystal Beach Park after Josephine Blanchat's death in September 1952.

Thelma Calvert is pictured with her husband, Jim Calvert, in 1955. Jim Calvert was a former teacher and coach at Vermilion High School from 1929–1944. He went on to teach and coach at Euclid Central and Euclid High School in Euclid, Ohio, until 1969.

Eleanor Ryan is shown with her husband, Jimmy Ryan, in 1972. Jimmy Ryan assumed the position of manager of the park after George Blanchat passed away in December 1938. In addition, Jimmy was a Lorain policeman and then safety director of Lorain.

George and Josephine Blanchat's grandchildren, Tom (Eleanor and Jimmy's son), and Sandra and Marlene (Thelma and Jim's daughters), are shown here around 1948.

Here we are again, now Marlene Calvert Feldkamp and, Sandra Calvert Mueller, along with Tom Ryan in 1993.

The Early Years

SHADDUCK'S GROVE A NICE SUMMER RESORT. FOR THOSE SEEKING PLEASURE. BOATS, BOTH SAIL AND ROW. EVERY THING IN GOOD ORDER. BOARD CAN BE HAD AT REASONABLE RATES. GIVE US A CALL. Mrs. J. SHADDUCK. VERMILLION OHIO. —1874—

The stagecoach house and grove of George Shadduck is shown in an early advertisement. The ad below the picture reads: "Shadduck's Grove A nice summer resort for those seeking pleasure. Boats, both sail and row. Everything in good order. Board can be had at reasonable rates. Give us a call. Mrs. J. Shadduck. Vermilion, Ohio."

The number of horse and buggies increased as Shadduck's Grove became more popular.

In 1898, Vermilion resident George "Pete" Wahl added a tent carousel to Shadduck's Grove. Mr. Wahl was assisted by his wife, Catherine, and daughters, Annetta, Hattie, and Marjorie. He also operated the shooting gallery at Crystal Beach and a carousel and shooting gallery at Linwood.

This particular kind of carousel had a circular track laid on the ground. There was a device for moving the horses in a rocking motion instead of up and down. The device revolved on the circular track. It was rotated by a slender cable that fit into the rim of the revolving platform, which led to a small steam engine standing a few feet away. The rocking motion was imparted to the horses by the track wheels. The carousel had a canvas top, poles, and an organ. The bottom photo on the previous page was taken circa 1910. A peanut cart is in the foreground to the right.

Carousel companies began changing around the turn of the century. Allen Herschell, who made the 1898 carousel, formed the Armitage-Herschell Company. The company went out of business in 1902. Then the Herschell-Spillman Company started up in 1911. In the early 1900s, an invention by F. H. Savage and Company of England was becoming popular. It employed a series of crankshafts mounted in the upper part of the revolving frame that were geared to rotate when the machine was in motion. From these crankshafts, the horses were suspended in such a manner that a smooth, galloping motion was imparted to them. In 1907 W. F. Mangels of Coney Island improved upon this design. All the animals, horses, and chariots were wooden and beautifully hand-carved and accented with jewels by German craftsmen.

Shadduck's stagecoach home, in 1906, was now owned and lived in by George, Josephine, and Thelma Blanchat. The home was eventually used as a tourist home and a two-family rental property. Some of the families that rented the home over the years were the Joleffs, Shannons, Spokishes, and Elstens.

These are the Joleff brothers, Gary, Pete, and Buddy, with Marlene. A sister named Joy was born later.

Art Elsten, Jr., and his wife, Ethel, had five boys. They were Dick, Jimmy, Larry, Jerry, and Denny.

George Blanchat commissioned Vermilion resident Dave Miller in 1906 to build this home next door to the stagecoach house. The three Blanchats moved into the home in time for the 1907 opening of Crystal Beach's first season. In 1910, Eleanor Blanchat was born in this home. This full view of the outside of the home remained the same until 1965, except for added landscaping including a beautiful catalpa tree that would be planted to the left of the office porch steps. The large front porch offered many hours of enjoyment. While sitting on the front porch's wicker furniture, the family would visit with guests as they watched people arriving for the dances.

The home's interior underwent many changes. The home had been constructed of black walnut. There were fifteen rooms. Downstairs, if you entered through the front door, you would find a vestibule that led to a reading room surrounded by a beautiful, wood-paneled landing. Along the base of the landing were seats with glass fronts. The top of the seats could lift up, enabling you to get the books that were stored inside. The stairway to the upstairs was adjacent to this room. Originally there were wooden pillars that separated the reading room and living room from each other. The dining room had a blue marble, tile fireplace. The "pocket" doors that closed off each of the rooms would slide into the walls when not in use. The pillars, fireplace, and doors were removed in the 1940s. A kitchen, small washroom, and an office were also on this first floor. Gas lights were replaced with electric.

After George Blanchat's death, Thelma, Jim, Marlene, and Sandra lived in the home with Josephine. There was a coal-burning furnace that heated the home. It was fun to watch the coal truck pull up to the basement window. A chute was lowered through the window into the coal bin. The coal made quite a racket as it was sent from the truck to the basement. Upstairs were five bedrooms, a full bath, and a large sunroom, or sitting room. The sitting room was used as a playroom that was filled with Marlene and Sandra's toys. Midway down the upstairs hallway was the door to the attic. Though the attic was not a finished room, it was always fun to see what "treasures" could be found. A laundry chute to the basement offered many hours of enjoyment to Marlene, Sandra, and Tom. Tom and his parents lived in Lorain. They would come and stay each weekend during the summer. A back stairway spiraled around from the upstairs down to the kitchen. From the kitchen was another stairway leading to a large basement that extended under the entire house.

This shows the east side of the home with the attached garage. Inside the home, Josephine and Thelma hosted many card parties for the various clubs they belonged to and for the church. The garage would eventually be the site of Halloween parties for us grandchildren, which were great fun.

This was an early entrance to Crystal Beach around 1911.

Workers in the park were made up mainly of family, friends, and people from Vermilion. Carl Lesher, brother of Josephine Blanchat, is shown second from the left leaning against the post. George Blanchat is the first one seated in the second row, far left, just in front of his brother-in-law.

Workers shown in front of the bathhouse are Lawson Rumsey, second from the left; owner George Blanchat; and Clorinda Rumsey.

Shown here are picnickers, around 1910, enjoying a day at the park.

Crystal Beach frequently featured live entertainment for the public to enjoy, as shown here. A memorable act that occurred in 1948 was The Great Eugene. He performed a high-wire act for the visitors to Crystal Beach. He had previously performed this act in Cleveland where he had walked the high-wire for 380 feet across the Cleveland Stadium at a height of 125 feet.

In the hollow was the beer garden. This is how it appeared in 1906. A miniature train would later circle around this hollow behind the midway before it continued along the lakefront and returned to the station.

This is the dining hall, which was the remodeled beer garden.

The dance hall located near the dining hall was also in the hollow. Popular dances when our grandparents first opened the hall were square dances, waltzes, schottisches, and the two-step.

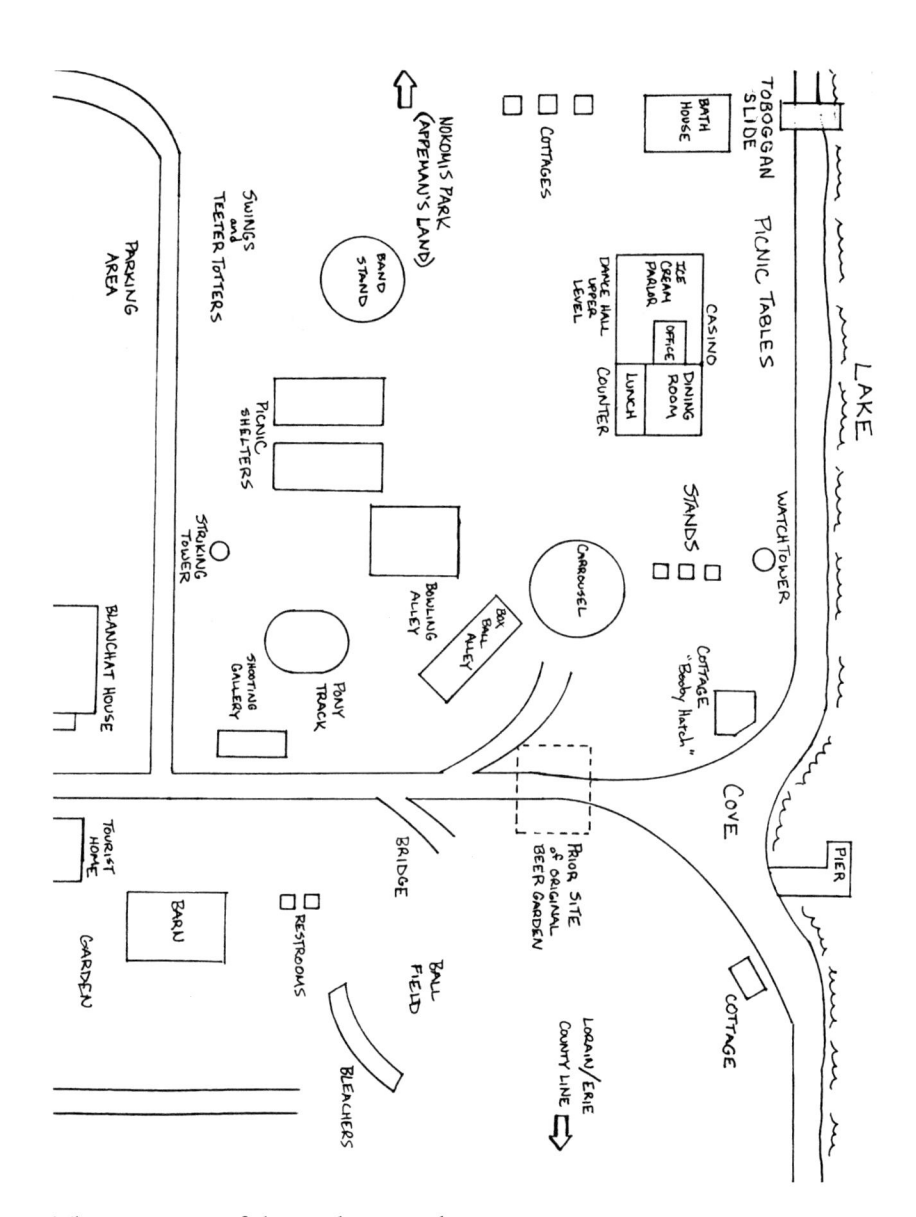

This is a map of the park around 1915.

Between 1907 and 1918, playground equipment, a bandstand, bowling and box-ball alleys, picnic shelters, bathhouses, a large arcade, and a toboggan to the lake were added. This shows the view of the entire toboggan. Rental boats are at the base.

Visitors watching the toboggan are perhaps trying to decide whether to climb the steps to the top. Due to the inclement weather of northeastern Ohio, George eventually decided to remove the toboggan.

This shows the end of the toboggan ride as it reaches the lake.

In 1910, Jim Dall gave rides from this dock to many visitors to the park in his boat, the *Edna D.* The boat was named after his wife. Here, bathers gather around the dock that leads to the *Edna D.*

Passengers board the *Edna D* for a ride.

Bathers enjoy the beach circa 1915. Though not in the picture, to the far left was the cove that led from the hollow to the lake and the boat dock. In the park's early years, eagles built a nest on the cliff. Cottages were built on each side of the cove. To the right in this picture is a signpost, which very faintly has the name *Edna D* to lead visitors to the boat ride.

For a time, boats could be rented. Visitors are seen here watching and waiting for a boat ride. The sign on the tree says "You can rent boats here."

A baseball field was on the east side of the hollow near the cottages. These bleachers were built so that people could sit and watch the games.

Here is one of the Crystal Beach baseball teams that George (middle row, second from the right) organized. Crystal Beach teams continued for quite a while. One of the park's opposing teams was the Jimmy Dulio Band.

Marlene remembers that she and Tom would often practice with the Crystal Beach team. In one practice game, played in the late forties, she was pitching. One of the men hit a line drive right to her.

He yelled to duck, but she caught it, to everyone's surprise. Though her hand stung and was red, she was pleased as the side was retired. During that practice game, Tom also made his mark by making a home run.

In 1909 a new pavilion and arcade building was constructed along the lakefront. The lower level of the 1909 pavilion offered a completely screened-in porch; a beautifully decorated, tea garden restaurant; and a private family dining room. The lower level also had an ice cream parlor; a large, open, short-order counter-type restaurant that offered hot and cold food; several souvenir stands; and the general office.

A dance hall with verandas encircling it was on the upper floor of the 1909 pavilion. The lake side of the ballroom was T-shaped and allowed for relaxing between dances and enjoying refreshments. A few years later, a ladies' bathhouse was built beneath it.

The ballroom had benches along the railings and elevated benches around the outer area to enable mothers to watch their children dance.

The first band to play in the ballroom was a group of Lorain and Elyria men, the Heinee Rembach Orchestra. It was a five-piece band consisting of Heinee Rembach on violin, Harry Slaughter on drums, Frank Horn on trumpet, Bill Rieth on trombone, and Rudy Koran (who married Vermilionite Alice Rumsey) on piano.

House bands were employed in the early twenties. These bands were usually college groups that were paid a flat salary plus room and board in the spacious dining room on the lower level.

The park charged five cents a dance. There were two large frames, one at either end of the hall, with slots in them. As the orchestra changed dances, cards were placed into the slots to announce what type of dance would be played next. Dances such as the waltz, two-step, and fox-trot were popular. When the shutters of the ballroom were opened, dancers enjoyed a pleasant lake breeze from all sides.

This view of the pavilion is the south or front view. The merry-go-round is just visible on the right. The penny arcade was on the far left of the lower level, then the tea garden restaurant, and the short-order counter. The dance hall and roller rink were upstairs. Eventually, the arcade became the total area left of the stairway, and the area to the right of the stairway continued to be the short-order counter.

Postcards were very popular. This one shows eight pictures of the park.

This postcard shows the beach with an inset of the new dance hall and entrance.

Here is an early advertisement of the park.

Crystal Beach
The Park of a Thousand Trees

An Ideal Place for Pleasure

VERMILION ~ ~ OHIO

Ed and Clara Neiding were very good friends of George and Josephine Blanchat. Ed was involved in operating the casino and played an important role in many other areas affecting the park. Clara sold tickets at the ballroom and helped at the bathhouse.

Ed Neiding was the first of three generations of Neidings to work at the park.

He was very well thought of and respected. A surprise birthday party was given for him in the new ballroom. He was told there was an electrical problem that needed his attention. Upon entering the dark building, he found the power switch and remarked, "All you need to do is turn the switch on." As he flipped the lights on, the gathered crowd yelled, "Surprise!"

Ed's son, Conrad "Coonie" Neiding, along with Coonie's son, Jerry, were all part of the Crystal Beach family.

Another of Ed's sons, Harold, is shown here with his wife, Sylva. Harold helped at the refreshment counter in the casino. He gave roller-skating lessons at the rink above the casino and was also a policeman. Sylva sold tickets at the front entrance to the ballroom.

Harold and Sylva's son, Jim, was, like Jerry, a third-generation Neiding that worked at the park. Although Jim was too young to be employed at the park, he came to help out his dad. Jim remembered his grandfather, Ed Neiding, telling him about the buckets of draft beer that were sold at the casino. The buckets would hold four glasses worth of beer and were sold for ten cents a bucket.

The park was a very safe and secure place. There was never a holdup or robbery. George and Ed would often close the pavilion by the lake. After midnight they would turn off all the lights and walk unbothered to the house with the evening receipts in a satchel. Even though the park was pitch black, George seemed to know where all the trees were. The receipts were counted the next morning in the Blanchat home at their dining room table. They were often taken to the bank in town by Thelma (right) and her cousin from Millersburg, Dot Nye (left). They are seen riding to town in Thelma's pony cart.

The Chandler Motor Car Company of Cleveland had a picnic on July 2, 1916. The company had only been in operation for three years. The picnickers all came to the park by autos. At that time, a seven-passenger car sold for $1,295. Chandler's slogan was "A parade of Chandlers built by the men who know."

As picnics began to flourish, many people began coming to the park by special train. The park had its own spur on the New York Central and Nickel Plate Railroads to accommodate those who did not come by horse and buggy or auto. An iron stairway led up from the tracks. The Lakeshore Electric Interurban also ran parallel to the New York Central, and a large waiting room was erected for the picnickers' protection. This is the old Lakeshore Interurban at stop 128.

Picnickers are coming to enjoy a day at Crystal Beach. Some may have used the wide gravel path that led from the shelter at the railroad to Lake Road and then to the park. Perhaps they even followed one of the bands that sometimes paraded down the path to the park. Eleanor remembered that when she and Thelma were little, they would call out, "The picnic is coming, the picnic is coming."

When reaching the park, picnickers could select from the various shelters available to set up their meals.

On the left is the bandstand in one of the entertainment sections in the center of the park. Dancers, who had been doing the two-step, waltz, and schottisches in the old dance hall, were now changing over to the jazz age. People were coming from the cities to enjoy the many summer cottages that surrounded Vermilion.

In the early 1900s the popcorn stand was a popular place in the park.

These are some of Eleanor's memories of the park's early days when she was a young girl.

The park was open every day and closed in the evenings. The dance hall closed promptly at 10:30 PM.

Before Christmas, George would get out his little black book and decide what companies he would call on to hold their picnics at the park. Mr. Humphreys of Euclid Beach and Mr. Boeckling of Cedar Point would meet in the Blanchat home. Together they would make plans for the coming season and decide on which picnics each of them would be hosting. George would then start his appointments with the companies in January.

Mr. and Mrs. Robert Pulley (Robert is shown here) were loyal to the park. The couple managed the dining room. They would often decorate it with fresh boughs of leaves and flowers. Mrs. Pulley was a superb cook. Mr. Pulley was a former porter for the New York Central Railroad.

The old movies featuring William S. Hart and other popular stars of the time were shown on a huge screen in the park. The lake flies looked like giants when the lights attracted them to the screen.

Lightweight Johnny Kilbane, who had been born in Cleveland, trained in the park for one of his fights. Jimmy Dunn was his manager. People came from miles around to see the great champion Kilbane.

The "big event" each year for Thelma and Eleanor was the arrival of the salesmen, who would come to their home to show George (who, at that time, ran the concessions) their merchandise for the stands. Items from kewpie dolls to bathing suits would be displayed. Each salesman would arrive bearing a gift for the girls.

The ponies were exercised and taken for a swim in the lake.

At one of the picnics, Thelma and Eleanor followed a short, stocky man who was dressed as a Bavarian. He would unbutton his vest, turn on a faucet, and fill picnickers' cups with beer. They finally guessed that his huge tummy must be a "pony," or small keg, of beer that was beneath his vest.

The Golden Years

This is the view in the early 1920s going east on Lake Road toward Crystal Beach. This is prior to the building of the ballroom.

The beautiful "Crystal Gardens" ballroom would be built on this large area of land to the west of the Blanchat home. The land was used as a parking lot before the building of the ballroom.

Crystal Gardens opened in 1925. Built by Dave Miller of Vermilion, the large, oval, steel building had a domed roof and matched, maple flooring. Bands played music such as "Twenty-three Skidoo," "So's Your Aunt Tillie," and "Razz-a-ma-tazz." Some dances popular at that time were the Black Bottom, the Charleston, and the Varsity Drag. Admission for the opening was ten cents. Dancing cost five cents a dance.

The Coon-Sanders Band was the first to play in the new ballroom. The band had been formed in 1919 in Kansas City. Carleton Coon and Joe Sanders were among the first bandleaders to discover the importance of radio for promoting their bands. Since their band broadcasted nightly on the radio at such a late hour, they took the nickname the "Nighthawks." In the '30s, Carleton Coon was killed in a car accident. The band, under the Joe Sanders name, continued to be popular.

Other bands to play in the ballroom in the early days were Fletcher Henderson, Paul Whiteman, Henry Busse, Vincent Lopez, and Ben Bernie.

Here is the front view of the ballroom along Lake Road. The ballroom was very spacious. After paying admission at the front door, people walked up ramps on either side to enter the ballroom. They would then go around the aisles between the rows of tables. Tables could be found along the railing of the dance floor, a popular choice, or near the window, where it was cooler. If a table wasn't available, people sat or stood on the benches against the walls to see the band. If you weren't early enough, and the benches were taken, you might have to stand by the railing at the north end of the dance hall.

This is another view of the Crystal Beach Ballroom. This one was taken from the Blanchat home next door.

Also a view from our home, this photograph was taken from the upstairs front window. Cars are arriving for a dance.

The parking lot within the park grounds can be seen behind the house. The midway is directly beyond the cars.

This view of the ballroom shows an earlier bandstand. At the railing openings are the stools for the ticket takers and the rectangular receptacles for the tickets. Hank Fisher, of Vermilion, who was ninety-three years old as of this writing, remembered taking tickets at the dance hall. He also remembered the employees wearing red tee-shirts with the initials "C. B." on them. In the previous picture, tables and chairs have not yet been added. The streamers from the lights, and, of course, the crystal ball, would remain permanent fixtures of the ballroom.

On warm nights, with all the windows open, the sound of the music could be plainly heard throughout our home next door. It is pleasant to recall the many evenings we spent sitting on the office porch swing of our home and listening to the sounds of the bands, the people's laughter, muffled voices, and the clinking sound of glasses. (There were no paper cups in those days.)

If people came into the ballroom through the entrance facing the park, they would see the souvenir stand, coat room, and park office on the left. Jerry Neiding of Vermilion and Chick Gracie of Lorain were workers at the coat check during some of the dances. Burt and Eleanor Hollosy frequently handled taking admissions at this entrance to the ballroom. Burt remembered standing outside the ballroom listening to the music one evening with a friend when he was a young man. Mr. Blanchat came by and gave them both tickets to get into the dance. On the right of the entrance was the refreshment counter.

Before going up the wide ramp to the ballroom, dancers may have seen George Villa of Vermilion (at far left) or Marie Smith, mother of Denny Smith of Brownhelm (far right), at the refreshment counter. Here they are taking time to have a little fun while awaiting the opening of the doors for that evening's dance.

Seen here at Jimmy and Eleanor's fiftieth wedding anniversary party are Marlene, Mary Robinson, Jim, and Joe Villa. Joe, as well as his brother, George, often worked at the ballroom and at the refreshment counter in the casino. Mary Robinson, of Lorain, was a good friend of the family who helped prepare meals in our home on Sundays. She was a wonderful cook. Mary's fried chicken and biscuits were absolutely the best.

This shows a later view inside the ballroom. This bandstand had a backstage area where the orchestra members could change. The bandstand remained the same until the park's closing. The front of the bandstand's lower tier was remodeled in 1960 so it could be removed when the ballroom was used for roller-skating and replaced when needed for the dances.

Dancing started at 9 PM and ended at 1 AM. Joe Trifiletti, a Lorain policeman, and Bill Virgin, a marine diver, were bouncers for the dance hall. They easily took care of any rowdy customers. During the 1930s and 1940s many big bands came to the Crystal Beach Ballroom. They not only brought their wonderful music, but they also left behind some interesting memories. The bandleader Les Brown who had the slogan "Les Brown and His Band of Re-known," featured Doris Day as his vocalist before she became more famous as a film star. Tom remembered having a Coke with her.

When Sammy Kaye appeared, he would let the audience have a try at directing the band. The selected participants would receive a baton for their efforts. His slogan was "Swing and Sway with Sammy Kaye."

All the bandleaders were very nice, but Jimmy remembered Tommy Dorsey as being the friendliest among them. There was not much time between the bands' arrivals and their performances, but Tommy would come down to the office an hour before the show to visit with Josephine. He would continue to play as long as there were people who stayed to listen. Then after the show he would come down and sit and talk until we closed. Marlene remembered Tommy reading a bedtime story to her. Her sister, Sandra, listened to the story while sitting on his lap.

ADVANCE TICKET
STAN KENTON
And His Orchestra
CRYSTAL BEACH
SUNDAY, MAY 16th, 1948
Advance Price $1.50, Tax Included
Nº 1853

Just as Tommy did, Stan Kenton, would come to our home before his performances. Each often stayed and visited with us on the side porch that faced the ballroom.

Vaughn Monroe broke attendance records at the ballroom, drawing a crowd of three thousand four hundred people. He had a beautiful voice. One of his big recordings at that time was "Ghost Riders in the Sky."

Ray Anthony's appearance matched Monroe's for crowd appeal; three thousand four hundred people were in attendance at his show as well. When Ray Anthony was at Crystal Beach in 1955, he called actress Mamie Van Doren in California to plan their wedding. She flew here, and they were married in Toledo.

Other famous bandleaders brought famous people to the ballroom throughout the years. Peggy Lee came to see Harry James, and Abbie Lane came with Xavier Cugat. Besides listening to Cugat, Lane also rode the rocket ships and went to the movies in Vermilion.

From the mid 1920s through the early 1960s, more than 150 bands graced the ballroom's bandstand. Some of the more well-known bandleaders performing at the park were Louie Prima, whose vocalist was Keely Smith; Louis Armstrong; Duke Ellington; Frankie Carle; Gene Krupa; Woody Herman; Guy Lombardo; and Count Basie.

An early 1930s band that played at the park, which perhaps was not as well known, was Chick Webb. His vocalist, however, became quite well known. She was Ella Fitzgerald.

Lawrence Welk played here many times before going on to Hollywood and hosting his own television show.

Pee Wee King was our first country band.

On Wednesday nights, we featured polka bands. Frankie Yankovic, "The Polka King," was one of the performers.

Later, when singing groups started to become popular, groups such as the Four Freshmen, the Four Lads, the Diamonds, the Everly Brothers, and the Kingston Trio appeared at the ballroom. Sandra remembers watching from the office porch next door as people gathered outside the windows of the ballroom to see the Kingston Trio. The inside of the ballroom had reached its capacity. The people who could not get in were standing three to four rows deep, completely surrounding the outside of the ballroom.

Bandleader Ralph Flanagan of Lorain took piano lessons from Lorain resident Harry Bomba. Flanagan is pictured on the next page with Eleanor and Jimmy Ryan in the park office before one of his performances. Thelma, Eleanor, and later Marlene and Tom, spent many hours in the park office. Tom remembered making change for the various operators who worked for the stands, rides, and refreshment places that the park owned. This included the dance hall, the casino, the shooting gallery, the Thriller, the kiddie rides, the Bug, the Ferris wheel, the rockets, the Laff-In-The-Dark, the Tilt-A-Whirl, and the miniature train. Ride operators would pick up their individual change bags and customer tickets each day and return them each evening for us to count. There were no checks or credit cards, just cash. The honor system worked as we never had to worry about the honesty of the individuals picking up the money.

In the early 1930s, bands were hired by the week and Sunday afternoon. At one time admission ranged from thirty to forty cents, and dances were free on Friday nights. Jimmy Dulio's band, as seen here, was from Lorain, and the band played at Crystal Beach from the early thirties until the park's closing season.

In later years, the local bands played only on Friday and Saturday nights. Friday night was singles night. Saturday night was date night. The name bands played on Sundays. Other local bands that started around the same time as Jimmy Dulio's band were the Campus Owls and Heinz-Billings. From Cleveland came Tommy Tucker, George Duffy, Ralph Webster, and Joe Baldi and his accordion.

During the Depression in 1932, dancers had a hard time getting enough money to pay for both gas and the dancing, even at a penny a dance. Campers' Night became very popular because all rides were half price and dancing was free every Friday night. In 1933 the ballroom was converted into a romantic garden. Soft lights, palm trees, floral decorations, and festoons of balloons adorned the dance hall. Tables and chairs were added, and floor shows were featured in addition to dancing.

Many activities continued to take place in the old dance hall over the casino. At one time there was a miniature golf course which had been designed by George. A Walkathon was held in 1934, and roller-skating remained popular. Appearances by celebrities, however, took place in the new ballroom.

Some of the big bands and orchestras that appeared at Crystal Beach from 1925 through 1960 were:

Coon-Sanders and the Nighthawks	Cab Calloway
Toad Rollines	Allan "Curly" Smith
Jan Savitt and "The Top Hatters"	Dick Stabile
Barney Rapp	Jan Garber
Johnnie Hamp	George Hall
Everett Hoagland	Russ Morgan
Emerson Gill	Chick Webb with Ella Fitzgerald
Herbie Kay	Al Kavelin

Henry Busse	Red Norvo
Les Brown with Doris Day	Dick Barrie
Fred Bergin	Bunny Berigan
Charles Stenross	Maurice Spitalny
Sal Cummings	George Williams
George Duffy	Ace Brigode
Tommy Tucker	Maurie Sherman
Ben Pollack	Gene Beecher
Brad Hunt	Jess Stacy
Orrin Tucker	Bob Strong
Will Osborne	Ray Anthony
Bob Chester	Ted Fio Rito
Leighton Noble	Jimmy Joy
Ina Rae Hutton	Benny Strong
Art Jarrett	Buddy Morrow
Vaughn Monroe	Johnny Long
Frankie Masters	Freddie Schaeffer and his all girl band
Sammy Kaye	Glenn Garr
Ray McKinley	George Olsen
George Towne	Sherman Hayes

Tommy Reed	Ray Bobbins
Randy Brooks	Bill Bardo
Dean Hudson	Russ Carlyle
Elliot Lawrence	Carmen Cavallaro
Chris Cross	Skitch Henderson
Stan Kenton	Charlie Fisk
Lee Castle	Lawrence Welk
Hal McIntyre	Tex Beneke
Tony Pastor	Ted Weems
Tommy Dorsey	Jimmy Dorsey
Blue Barron	Shep Fields
Tommy Carlyn	Frankie Carle
Larry Clinton	Frankie Yankovic
Charlie Spivak	Alvino Rey
Claude Thornhill	Victor Lombardo
Teddy Phillips	Guy Lombardo
Chuck Foster	Eddy Howard
Xavier Cugat	Sonny Dunham
Larry Fontine	Woody Herman
Duke Ellington	Louis Armstrong
Count Basie	The Diamonds

Ray Robbins	Ralph Flanagan
Harry James	Gene Krupa
Buddy Laine	Charlie Barnet
Louis Prima	Jerry Gray
Bill Lawrence (star of *Arthur Godfrey Show*)	Billy May
Lee Barrett	Neal Hefti and Frances Wayne
Joy Cayler and her all girl orchestra	Griff Williams
Pee Wee Hunt	Ralph Marterie
Russ Romero	Paul Neighbors
Sauter and Finegan	Pee Wee King
The Gaylords	Ernie Rudy
The Four Lads	Les Elgart
Richard Maltby	The Four Freshmen
The Everly Brothers	The Kingston Trio
Jimmy Dulio	Chuck Bizgrove

Advertisements like that on the following page appeared first in our local newspaper, *The Vermilion News*. Eleanor would do the layout and write the copy for all the ads. She would also use her artistic ability each week to create large signs promoting the next week's attraction. The hand-painted signs were made on a tagboard backing. Glitter surrounded the photos of the celebrity bandleader and singer. She made as many as twenty signs a summer. Unfortunately, none of her beautiful creations remain.

Below is *The Vermilion News* building in which all the park's tickets, handbills, and posters were printed. Marlene remembered going with our mother to turn in articles for the next week's events. Pearl and Bessie Roscoe were the owners of *The Vermilion News*. The Roscoes were always helpful and gracious. Their daughter, Ella Roscoe Tarrant, and her husband, William, took over the business with their children Bill, Nancy, Richard, and Albert. Though the building is no longer used as a newspaper office, the interior remains the same. For those of us who spent time in *The Vermilion News* headquarters, a return visit was like stepping back into the past. Albert and Richard Tarrant continue to be active in preserving the building as a part of Vermilion history. Richard Tarrant's desire to preserve the history of Vermilion is also evident with the publishing of his interesting narrative on Crystal Beach Park. The narrative can be found online (http://www.geocities.com/vermviews/crystalbeach.html).

Albert Tarrant gave us these original tickets for the Roller Gardens. They were a welcome memento for our collection.

Thelma and Josephine pose in front of the new Thriller in 1926. Thelma became a teacher at Vermilion High School a year after this picture was taken. She taught business and commercial subjects for nine years until she got married. In those days, married women could not continue teaching. Thelma handled the bookkeeping duties of the park and helped to get picnics. Living in the Blanchat home allowed her access to the daily needs that required immediate attention.

There were two types of roller coasters in 1925. They were the underslung and the channel ride. At the time of negotiations, George was asked what type he wanted. His reply was, "the safest." So

50

it was the channel ride, which was the safest and most costly to maintain, that was constructed. On November 20, 1925, Toledo Beach Toboggan Company of Pittsburgh, Pennsylvania, and George Blanchat entered into an agreement, which stated that Blanchat would "lease for a period of ten years a location in the park to be selected by both parties for the building and operation of a gravity ride." The location of the gravity ride needed to be on a space of ground ninety feet by three hundred feet.

The Thriller, as it was called, was completed and ready for the opening of the park on May 30, 1926. The ride was owned by the T. M. Harton Co. of Pittsburgh when it was purchased by the park in 1949.

This is a view of the Thriller at the beginning of the ride. Frank Kish and Henry Rust were longtime operators of the ride. Julia Kish, Frank's wife, would often be a cashier for the Thriller.

We're on our way to the highest point of the ride, which was sixty-one feet. The car could travel seventy miles per hour in the dips. It took one minute to get to the top of the first incline.

What a view at the top—for a moment! The ride lasted two and a half minutes at the beginning of the season. Later, when the ride was running smoother, it lasted one minute and fifty-five seconds. In ten years, the Thriller carried one million seven hundred fifty thousand people. Shown here is a view of the twenty acres south of Lake Road in the mid-1950s before the shopping center was built. The coaster had two thousand three hundred feet of track and used two hundred thousand board feet of lumber. It was built from Alabama pine. There were no knots in any of the boards. The insurance company did not permit the wood to ever be painted, as paint would hide any defects in the wood.

We always knew it was spring when we heard the purr of the tractor that meant Elmer Neiding was mowing the field to prepare it for parking and the sound of the clickity-clack of the roller coaster. Elmer, Ed Neiding's son, also worked as a policeman at the park.

Every spring "the rust removing crew," as seen on the next page, would set about to work. Paul Reis, Henry Rust, and Jimmy Ryan would use one car and two oil cans as they made many trips on the gravity-powered ride to remove any rust accumulation from the winter. The rust would cause a drag at the under and side wheels. This prevented "sway" by pressing against the side boards. When the car stuck, safety locks caught the car, and the fellows would hop out and push the car, one leg in and one leg out, like a scooter. When the car took off they would jump into the car and ride along until the next "stalling." Sound like fun?

The operators walked the ride every day during the season, checking for any defects. If any were found, they were corrected immediately. Russ Dickerhoff of Vermilion remembered many days when he and Roberta Reis, Paul's daughter, would ride in the front car of the coaster helping to check the smoothness of the ride as it took the turns. The ride was thoroughly inspected every year by an inspector of the U.S. Fidelity Guarantee Insurance Company. The inspector worked from early morning till late in the day checking the entire structure.

A familiar sight on the grounds was the truck that was used for clean up, picking up blocks of ice from Vermilion, and many other jobs. Tom remembered driving this truck to pick up trash and take it to various dumps. One place was by Romp's property, and another by the water tower. He also remembered driving to the ice house owned by Harry Hayes, which was located near the bridge going into town. There he would get the one hundred to six hundred pounds of ice needed to cool the pop and beer at the casino and ballroom. There were no electric coolers at that time.

Tom also remembered that during World War II, he would collect whiskey bottles from the park grounds, which he would sell for a penny a piece to the "break the bottle" stand, and cigarette packs so he could remove the tin foil liner and make balls of tinfoil to give to the war effort.

This is a view from our back porch that shows the batter's cage. The cage was one of the many additions to the park, which continued to grow over the years, adding fifteen major rides; seven kiddie rides; pony rides, two athletic fields, a fun house, a miniature golf course, an arcade with skeeball, and a strike and spare alley; a photo gallery; and a penny arcade. Eventually, there were twenty-eight concessions, six different refreshment stands, a restaurant, a tourist home, and fifteen cottages.

The park sponsored home shows, boxing shows, and free acts. In addition, it offered to the general public free parking and the use of picnic facilities and the beach. There was a free fireworks show set up in the hollow each Fourth of July. Our family would sometimes watch the fireworks from the window at the end of the hallway upstairs. A favorite display of Sandra's was named the Niagara Falls.

Unlike amusement parks today, the admission to the park was free. The ride operators or the cashiers would handle the money and tickets for each ride. As a cashier, Sandra remembers cashiering at the kiddie rides, the Bug, and the Laff-In-The-Dark.

Rides cost ten cents, fifteen cents, or twenty-five cents. The park opened in the evening during the week between 6 and 7 PM and closed between 11 PM and midnight. It was open on Sunday from 1 PM until 10 PM. Saturdays were generally reserved for company picnics.

Here is an advertisement for a free act offered to Crystal Beach visitors.

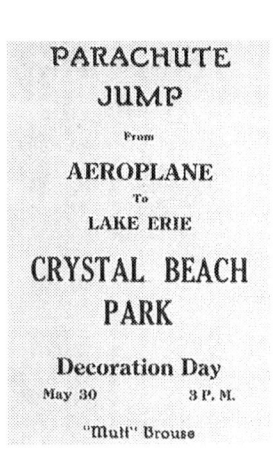

PARACHUTE
JUMP
From
AEROPLANE
To
LAKE ERIE
CRYSTAL BEACH
PARK
Decoration Day
May 30   3 P. M.
"Mutt" Brouse

The pony rides were between the arcade and the train station. George purchased the ponies from Bud Mc Queen, who lived nearby. Pony rides for youngsters were always fun. This photograph was taken in the forties before a fire completely destroyed the original arcade that can be seen in the background.

A popular ride for those with strong stomachs was the Tilt-A-Whirl.

The Tumble Bug, or Bug, would always have long lines during picnics.

This shows Marlene, Sandra, and Thelma taking some time to enjoy a ride on the Bug.

Art Smith, one of the operators of the ride, was the park's only full-time, year-round employee. Dan Van Fossen and Henry Rust were also Bug operators. Dan Van Fossen had a day job as a welder. His skill as a welder helped us out considerably as he was able to repair many a ride for us. Eva Blattner often cashiered here, and she sold tickets during picnics.

The Caterpillar is shown here in front of the Dodgem.

This was the Silver Streak.

Another ride was the Octopus.

The Spitfire was located next to the casino.

This is an early model of the miniature train in the depot. The first train was fueled by coal.

The trains were later steam, gasoline, and then diesel powered. Darlene Villa, Joe Villa's daughter, worked at the train depot.

Tom and his mother, Eleanor, wait for the train ride to begin. Perhaps they are listening to the engineer calling, "Down around the lakefront, through the park, and back again. Great big ride on a little train, only fifteen cents."

For a short time, after World War II, the hollow was the site of an unusual ride. Two local GIs named Joe Yelensky and Oswald Kelm brought an amphibious duck, like this one, to the park and gave rides on it from the cove into the lake.

Here is an early picture of the carousel.

This is a later picture of the carousel, now renamed the merry-go-round. Mary Shuman and her two daughters, Barbara Shuman Hunter and Mary Ann Shuman Carroll, owned and operated the ride. The Shumans were the only other family that owned rides in the park. Carousel rides cost ten cents a ride for children and fifteen cents for adults. The ride had many beautifully hand-carved animals and horses. The organ played many tunes, but the one that we most vividly remember is "A Bushel and a Peck." One of the cashiers for the ride was Lucy Hess. For one summer David Feldkamp worked at the merry-go-round. He later assisted Jim in running the rocket ships. Several years later, he and Marlene would marry.

Mary Ann and Barbara Shuman pose for this picture in the mid 1940s.

Marvelee and Pat Malcomson stand in front of the lakefront pavilion. A nice view of the merry-go-round is in the background.

These are some examples of Herschell-Spillman animals from the carousel. They are the cat, goat, and rooster. The animals that went around the outside like the giraffe, lion, tiger, deer, and ostrich were stationary. At one time there had been a dragon, but it was removed because it scared the children. The Herschell-Spillman Company was known for creating a wide variety of menagerie figures for its rides.

There were beautiful panels surrounding the center part of the carousel. We vividly remember two of them. One represented the Vermilion River where the soil was red and where Indians lived. The other showed the lake with sailboats and fishing boats. Both represented specific features of the Vermilion area. They were hand-painted by traveling artists.

This shows a section of the inside of the merry-go-round as Barb Shuman operates the ride.

The Ferris wheel was located next to the dance hall and rockets on the west side of the park near the entrance.

The seaplanes preceded the rockets. They had "Lindbergh" written on the sides.

The rocket ships were a gift to Thelma and Jim from George and Josephine. Jim spent many a day caring for and running the rockets. He is pictured at the upper-right hand corner. Jim also took care of the landscaping around the family home and in front of the dance hall.

64

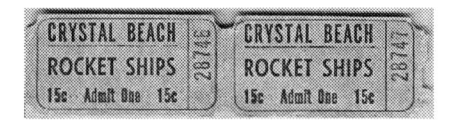

These tickets were given to us by Joan and Barry Lima, who had saved them as a remembrance of the fun times they had spent at Crystal Beach Park.

The sign to the entrance was adjacent to the Nakomis property near Lake Road.

This Loop-O-Plane was better known as the "Hammers." At one time, Francis Dean from Vermilion-on-the-Lake and his son, Jim, owned and operated this ride. Dean had purchased it from the Shumans around 1951.

This view of the Loop-O-Plane shows the sidewalk leading north towards the casino.

If you followed the path in the opposite direction, you would arrive at the dance hall.

The Laff-In-The-Dark in this picture is under construction. It was built where the storeroom that was destroyed in the fire of 1947 had stood.

In this picture, the Laff-In-The-Dark is now open for business. This ride had lots of twists and turns. Bob Braden and Ray Beursken, both of Vermilion, were two former operators of the ride. As kids, we had fun when the operators turned the lights on and let us ride through so we could see what all those scary things really looked like.

Mary Shuman and her daughters, Barbara and Mary Ann, owned and operated the dodgem. The Shumans purchased the ride from the Malcomsons in the early forties. The dodgem was located on the west side of the park. It cost twenty-five cents a ride.

Mary Ann Shuman is shown here in the early 1960s.

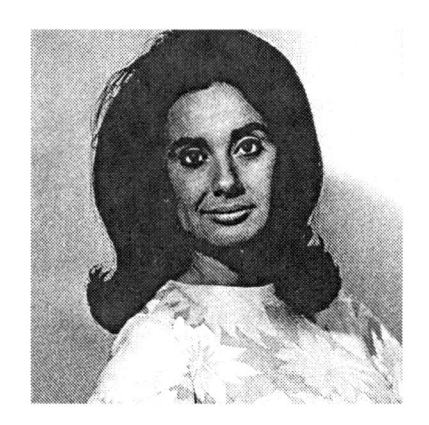

Barbara Shuman is pictured here in 1958.

Mary Shuman and her husband, Jack Shuman, came to the park around 1942. The Shumans at one time were owners of the rifle range at the park. They also owned, at various times, roller rinks at Ruggles Beach, Cable Block in Sandusky, Elberta Beach, Rye Beach, Buckeye Lake, and the rink above the lakefront pavilion at Crystal Beach. Jack passed away in 1944. As a widow with two small children, Mary was ahead of her time as a woman competing in the business world, capably handling all that came her way.

Jack Shuman is shown here in the late 1930s.

Here are Mary Shuman and Elma Edge. Elma lived in Nakomis and played the organ at local skating rinks.

The basketball toss and the archery stands were on the west side of the park between the Dodgem and the Laff-In-The-Dark. John Hartman had the archery stand. The basketball toss was for a time owned and operated by John Brackley. He later sold it to Bob Hunter.

Bob and Barbara Shuman Hunter had the Guess-Your-Age-and-Weight stand just outside the front of the casino. Bob also ran the penny pitch on the midway side of the park.

A stand located next to the basketball toss was "Trickee." It involved standing up bottles using a fishing pole with a ring attached to the line. Ann and Frank Whitman, their son, Bill Whitman, and their niece, Anna Marie Sullivan Jones, owned and ran Trickee.

Anna Marie's younger sister, Arlene Sullivan, received a special treat when the Everly Brothers came to the park. She was able to go on the stage in the ballroom to have her picture taken with them and to get their autographs. Arlene was a former Miss Vermilion.

The Crazy House was dark inside with very narrow passageways that had lots of sharp turns leading into a topsy-turvy room. In this room, marbles ran uphill, and the floor was slanted. Outside was a moving sidewalk that allowed you a brief moment of light before returning you to the dark passageways. Blasts of air from the sidewalk urged you to hurry along. Tom and Marlene used to go through the Crazy House so many times that they would try various ways to proceed. Sometimes they would go through with their eyes closed, and sometimes they would race to see who could make it through first.

Paul Reis at one time managed the Crazy House, and his daughter, Cloris, was a cashier.

This was the miniature golf course, which was run and maintained by Charles and Margretta Fleming. It was situated just opposite the midway.

Margretta and her son Dick Fleming are shown here in the 1940s.

The kiddie rides were found between the dodgems and the train depot under the protection of many shade trees. There were five rides. Tom remembers being given the responsibility of operating all the kiddie rides. He hired the people to run the rides and to sell tickets. His right-hand man was Billy Burke. Carl Wetzel, Larry Gendics, Sonny Falls, and Kenny Kidd were others who worked at the kiddie rides. Tickets were ten cents each or three for a quarter. Tom's future wife, Carole Czech, sold tickets at the kiddie rides. Pictured is an earlier kiddie car ride with a canvas top.

The miniature Ferris wheel is run by Tom.

These are the kiddie boat rides.

The hand cars were a favorite with the children. If you got tired cranking the wheel, you could get help from the operator, Bill Boros, who is shown here.

These are the kiddie cars.

Here is the kiddie rocket ride.

Judy Murphy and Sandie Pheneger are standing between the kiddie rides and the dodgem.

The concession stands on the midway were located between the carousel and the rifle range on the east side of the park. There were a variety of games over the years. Some were spill the milk bottles, burst the balloons with darts, striker tower, penny pitch, the duck pond, bubble bounce, and bingo, to name a few. The concessions were family owned and operated. Individual families, both from the area and from other states, would return each summer. Some of the families were Art and Frances Elsten, William and Betty Gillis, Johnny and Pearl Smarsh, Dorothy Murphy, the Meiferts (Walter, Ellen, Dick, and Dave), and Ivan and Grace Murphy. The Murphys brought their four children, George, Ray, Deanie, and Judy, from Indiana. Their family returned to the park for over twenty years and remained an integral part of the Crystal Beach family.

The first stand on the north end of the midway near the merry-go-round was run by Johnny Krock. Sandra remembers playing this game of chance very well. You had to pull a ball attached to a cord, which allowed other small balls to fall through an arrangement of nails to spots below marked with numbers. If you got the right combination of numbers, the sum of which corresponded with one of the numbered shelves, you would win a prize. After many disappointing tries, she was able to "win" her panda, which she still has as of this writing.

This shows the midway as it continues southward toward the front of the park. The Murphy and Gillis families had their concessions in this section. George, Larry, Marty, and Shirley Gendics worked at the Murphys' stands. Directly across from here was the striker tower and the penny pitch.

These stands were the bubble bounce and duck pond, run by the Elstens and the Smarshes respectively.

Pictured here are Pearl Smarsh and Deanie Murphy, and Frances and Art Elsten. Pearl and Frances are sisters. The Elstens came to the park about the same time as the Murphys in the early forties.

Walter, Evelyn, Dick, and Dave Meifert ran this bingo stand.

This close-up of the bingo stand shows some of the prizes.

Paul Reis of Vermilion operated the rifle range, which was located at the end of the midway nearest the Thriller and across from the bingo stand. George Hoffman and Russ Dickerhoff of Vermilion were two workers at the rifle range. It offered twenty shots for a quarter. The concession was later sold to Dr. Paul Kopsch of Amherst in 1962.

This building next to the rifle range was used in a variety of ways. It was a photo booth that was run by Betty and Bill Harrington, and, at one time, it was a custard stand run by Pete and Minnie Derby with their daughter, Gloria. The Derbys were related to the Malcomsons, who ran the arcade. The building also served as a souvenir stand. The road that went through the park was on the right of this building. It led to the hollow and continued to where the cottages and ball field were located.

At one of the early concession stands, Mary George, a Rumanian gypsy, would tell fortunes, by reading palms and using a crystal ball. Mary, her husband, Jim, their son, Mike, and their daughter-in-law, Maria, all came to the park in 1921 from Chicago. Jim and Mike took very good care of the park grounds. They lived in one of the cottages, and paid their rent promptly, and always with gold pieces. The women wore beautiful chains of various gold coins and necklaces. They still clung to many of their old customs as to dress and rituals.

They had lost their life savings in the bank crash in Chicago during the Depression.

Diane George, Mary and Jim's granddaughter, was the last of the family to work at the park, and she did so until 1947. In 1957 the ballroom was the site of a double wedding of the son and his bride, and the daughter and her groom, of the king of the gypsies, Eli Ziko. He was the king of four states—Ohio, Indiana, Illinois, and Maryland. A huge crowd came both to participate and to watch. The banquet consisted of ducks, chickens, and five roasted pigs. It was an elaborate ceremony with many colorful costumes and dances.

In the late forties, Dorothy Murphy, pictured here, assumed the palmistry concession. Dorothy was married to Ike Murphy, who was Ivan Murphy's brother.

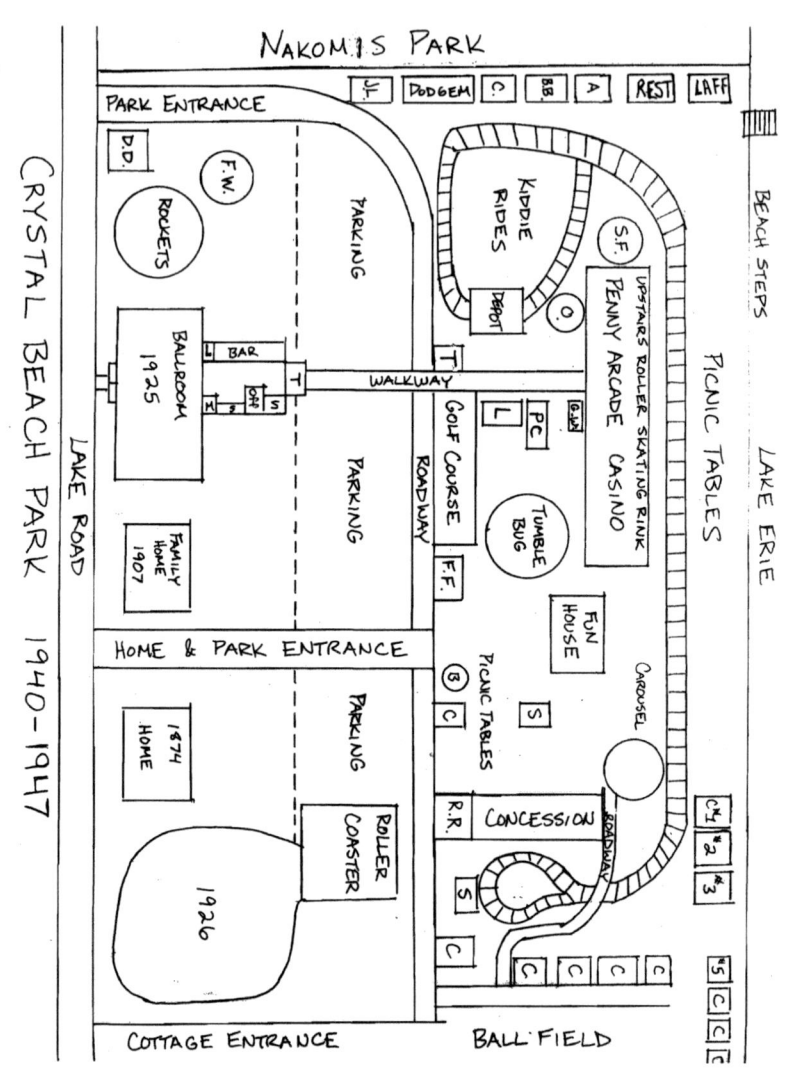

This is a map drawn to show what the park looked like sometime between 1940 and 1947, as well as a few additions of attractions from the 1950s. The key to the lettered places goes clockwise: (DD) Dari Delite, (FW) Ferris Wheel, (JL) Jungle Larry, (C) Trickee, (BB) Basketball Toss, (A) Archery, (Rest) Restroom, (Laff) Laff-In-The-Dark, (SF) Spitfire, (O) Octopus, (GW) Guess Your Weight, (PC) Popcorn Stand, (L) Loop, (T) Taffy, (FF) French Fry Stand, (B) Bingo, (S) Striker, (RR) Rifle Range, (S) Storage, (C) Cottages; Ballroom, (T) Tickets, (S) Souvenirs, and (Off) Office.

As the park entered into the '30s and '40s, many events were shaping its future. During the Depression, the picnic business suffered greatly from the Wagner Act (which would later be revised and known as the Taft-Hartley Act). The Wagner Act prohibited companies from giving picnics as a reward to their employees. Labor unions eventually took over the picnics, and the cost to the park for committee fees was great.

In December 1938, George passed away. His son-in-law, James, who had been active in the park business since 1929, became manager of the park for Josephine. This picture of Josephine was taken around 1950.

During the war years of 1941–1945, there was a shortage of gasoline, meat, and sugar. The park had to get as much sugar as possible to the Vermilion Bottling Company in order to ensure that enough pop would be available. Root beer, cherry, cream soda, and orange soda pop were made right in Vermilion on Ohio Street. The bottling company was once owned by Norbert Feldkamp, an uncle of David Feldkamp.

Meat markets such as Fligner's supplied the park's hamburgers. Martin's Market, owned and run by Steve and Margaret Martin, the parents of Marlene Martin Young of Vermilion, supplied hot dogs. Someone from the park would visit other meat markets and butchers for miles around to be sure there were enough hamburgers, hot dogs, and ham to fill the demand. Other local suppliers to the park included Ken and Jerry Goodman (beer); Dan Canalos (cigarettes, cigars, and candy); Pete Desantis (potato chips); and Maurer-Wikel (dairy products).

Beer was in very short supply. Often stock had to be purchased in a company for a dollar a share. There was also an extra dollar placed on each case over and above the price of the beer. All beer and pop bottles at that time were returnable. Tom remembers collecting empty beer and pop bottles in a wagon, bringing them back to an area to sort, and putting them into cases so the park could get the deposit credit from the suppliers. The biggest pop sellers at that time were Coca Cola, Seven-Up, and Orange. Marlene remembered helping stock the cases of pop for dances and picnics.

After the Fire

Just as the park's fortieth anniversary was approaching, a disastrous fire swept through the grounds on Sunday morning, April 20, 1947. According to Thelma's memory of the fire, Police Marshall Ed Benson was investigating a traffic accident in front of the ballroom at about 3:30 AM. He noticed a flash of lightning in the park. The next thing he knew, the whole second floor of the lakefront arcade was ablaze. The fire traveled on the electrical wires, and the flames rose over fifty feet. The Vermilion, Vermilion-on-the-Lake, Lorain, Huron, and Berlin Heights fire departments rushed to the scene. The fire lasted for five hours, melting several roofs of homes in Nakomis Park.

Though on site, not all of the fire departments could use their equipment because they could not get to the lake to supply the hydrants with water. Fortunately the wind shifted, and it started to rain. This helped save the park. Otherwise, the blaze might have shifted to the merry-go-round, which had a freshly painted roof. From there it could have traveled down the midway, spread to the Thriller, and the Blanchat home, and destroyed the entire park.

The fire had completely destroyed the lakefront pavilion and the park warehouse, where many rides and much equipment were stored. Picnic tables, lumber, tools, the roller-skating rink, the penny arcade, the refreshment casino, and the skeeball alleys could not be saved. The fire also destroyed several other buildings and more than twenty large shade trees. The cost of the destruction was estimated at 150 thousand dollars. The next day a continual procession of people came to view the destruction.

Both Thelma and Marlene had vivid memories of that April morning. Thelma had been awakened about 4:30 AM by a crackling sound. When she went to investigate, she looked out the hallway window, which faced the park. Her reaction to what she saw was, "My heart stood still as the whole park appeared to be ablaze." She then ran down the stairs, past Marlene, to call her brother-in-law,

Jimmy Ryan, who lived in Lorain. Within half an hour, he was at the park.

Marlene remembered awakening to the sound of the phone ringing. She saw a red glow coming from outside her bedroom window. When she went into the hallway to see what was happening, she glanced towards the same window that Thelma described looking out of. She ran to the window and saw a wall of flames the width of the park and as tall as the tallest trees. As she ran to her parents' room to tell them the park was on fire, she saw her mother racing down the stairs.

Here is one last view of the beautiful lakefront pavilion before it was burned.

In this photograph taken after the fire, the merry-go-round and the three cottages remain in stark contrast to the empty space where the arcade had once stood.

Workmen assemble the new casino and penny arcade on the same location that the 1909 pavilion had been before it burned. The one-story structure would be more modern. It had steel beams and a steel roof covered with eight-inch fiberglass insulation. It was very unlike the wooden structure that it replaced. The T.J. Hume Company built the new casino and arcade. It was completed in sixty days, just in time for the Fourth of July, at a cost of fifty thousand dollars.

This picture shows the front of the new casino and the Guess-Your-Weight stand. The arcade was on the west side, and the refreshment counter was on the east side next to the merry-go-round. Coonie and Jerry Neiding, along with George and Joe Villa, could often be found working behind the refreshment counter in the new casino. Tom remembered how they made hamburger patties from fresh ground beef. They would use an ice cream scoop to make the patties the right size. Then they'd place wax paper on the top and bottom of the meat. This would then be put in a press to make a "perfect" patty.

The Judge brothers pose in the photo booth in the arcade. They worked at the Guess-Your-Weight stand.

Inside the arcade were a variety of attractions to test the visitors' skills and to entertain. These machines gave advice and told fortunes. Behind them were the popular skeeball alleys. There were machines where you turned a crank, and pictures would flip to show silent movies. Sandra remembers watching one machine that showed the Hindenburg crashing in flames to the ground. She also remembers the evenings when many of the younger crowd that came to the park could be found dancing in the casino. The jukebox was filled with 45 rpm records that played music that reflected the new dance craze, rock and roll, and included dances like the jitterbug, the twist, and the stroll. If you didn't want to listen to music, you could make your own with the voice-o-gram. These machines would record your voice on a small record.

There were photo booths for taking many kinds of pictures. Some were pictures that could have a metal frame, as shown with Tom and his dad, Jimmy.

Another metal frame photo shows Sandra and her friend Nadine Mroski of Vermilion, whose family had a shoe store in town.

Bill and Betty Harrington were the park photographers. Many of the photos seen throughout this book with the special background were taken by them and supplied to us from George Murphy's collection.

Charlie Zoro worked in the arcade at the skeeball area.

Thelma and Roy Malcomson were owners and operators of the penny arcade equipment.

Patty and Marvelee Malcomson are Thelma and Roy's daughters.

Patty sits here with her future husband, Chuck Smith.

This shows the back of the casino that faced the lake. There were plenty of picnic tables for people to enjoy a meal or to just relax and watch the lake.

Another view behind the casino shows the miniature train tracks on the right and cottage 1 in the background.

A close up of cottage 1 shows Roy and Patty on their porch. The Malcomsons ran the arcade. They lived in this cottage during the summer, which made it easy to get to work. Patty remembers what great fun it was growing up at the park. Friends would often remark to her how lucky she was to be living at the park.

Along with the Malcomsons', there were fourteen other cottages. They were first rented by the week, but later on they were rented by the season. The cottages were fully furnished. Renters needed only towels, bedding, and food. Each cottage had an oak icebox. Concessioners like the Gillis family and the Murphy family lived in some.

Ivan and Grace Murphy came to the park in 1939. They came from Greentown, Indiana. Before operating concessions at Crystal Beach, the Murphys ran concessions at Joyland Park in Kentucky. During the off season, Ivan was a barber. In this photo Grace and Ivan are relaxing in their backyard in Greentown, Indiana. This was taken after the park closed.

George Murphy was the oldest of the Murphy children. He is responsible for many of the photos of people and places seen in this book.

Pictured are Ray Murphy and Thelma Dean Rust. Thelma married Henry Rust, operator of the Thriller and the Bug. She was the daughter of Mr. Dean, who ran the Loop-O-Plane.

Judy Murphy Branan with Betty Belle Harrington pose for this photo in the late 1940s.

This group photo was taken outside of the ballroom, and it shows some of the Crystal Beach family that our family can well recall and others whose names we can't quite place. In the first row are Mary Green, Betty Belle Harrington, Gloria Derby, Deanie Murphy, Lois Lumley, and Pee Wee Spaulding. In the second row, we are not sure of the first person. To his left is Patty Malcomson, Ray Murphy, Marvelee Malcomson, Dorothy Murphy, and Dick Fleming. The third row includes Charles Fleming, Thelma Malcomson, Margretta Fleming, Grace Murphy, and Ivan Murphy. On the fourth row the only person known for certain is Tony Perisi, who is in the center with one boy's arm over his shoulder. Included on the fifth row are Jim George, George Murphy, a gentleman we can't place, Red Bates, Roy Malcomson, and Paul Lafever.

These cottages were on the east side of the hollow. They were along the perimeter of where the ball field used to be.

These cottages were along the lake. Cottage 6 was one of the two biggest cottages. For many years, the Timm family occupied it. The expanse of land shown in front of these cottages was the site of many games and activities sponsored by the picnics that came to the park.

Picnics and Other Attractions

In the early days, the picnics had the typical games you might see now like races, ball games, tug of war, and various contests. There were, in addition, some unusual events that made the newspapers. According to an early article in *The Lorain Daily News* Friday, August 23, 1907, the Lorain merchants' picnic held a mule race, which was "the cause of considerable merriment." The article went on to say that the "mule race was one of the big features and the pair of 'Mauds' caused all kinds of amusement for the spectators. The mules seemed to know little about racing and were extremely bad about keeping on the road. One of the animals had a mania for jumping into the crowd and at other times hiking through a corn field that bordered the road."

As this same article continued, it related the outcome of the "fat man's race." One gentleman, who evidently was a politician, "surprised his friends and it is a cinch that if Charlie runs at half the clip for another term in the city council as he did yesterday he will win hands down."

A news article dated Friday, August 8, 1913, from *The Amherst News* shared the results of contests for the Amherst merchants, firemen, and Sunday school picnics. It read, "The nail driving contest for ladies furnished a good deal of amusement and they were cheered to put forth their best efforts."

There were contests for the shortest and tallest farmer and lady, and for the largest family. The winning family was the Bartholomews. The article stated, "When Fred Bartholomew of Brownhelm led forth his flock in the contest for the largest family, all the other contestants disappeared. Bartholomew and wife climbed on the stand with an even dozen children. He explained that they had a 'baker's dozen,' but one could not be present." For those not familiar with the term "baker's dozen," it means one more than a dozen, or one for the baker. Any way you look at it, that was a large family.

As the years went by, the park began getting more company-sponsored picnics. The annual farmer's picnic was held each Fourth of July. In the 1920s the First National Tube Company Picnic was held, and, despite a downpour, ten thousand people continued to have fun. The CIO, the AFL, Ford Motor Company, Bendix, Westinghouse, American Ship, Grafton Foundry, Larson Foundry, Freuhauf Trailer, White-Roth Manufacturing, Ohio Edison Company, and Western Automatic were a few of those who came to the park. Numerous picnics sponsored annually by factories, industries, businesses, organizations, churches, and communities were an important source of business for the park.

The CIO picnic of August 3, 1946, drew twenty-five thousand people to hear Congressman Walter Huber speak. The CIO picnic of Sunday, July 27, 1947, was even greater. It drew the largest crowd that ever was at Crystal Beach. There were ten thousand union members, thirty thousand people in all. This was the tenth annual picnic, and the CIO national president, Phillip Murray, was the guest speaker. The picnic was also highlighted by a fourteen-mile marathon race from the union hall in Lorain to the park, as well as a lavish beauty contest. Traffic was so heavy that day it caused the greatest traffic jam in the history of Vermilion. Cars were detoured down Baumhart and Sunnyside Roads to Brownhelm and then to Vermilion. Cars were parked along the highway as far as Vermilion-on-the-Lake. Traffic was backed up to Beaver Park.

The picnics were usually on Saturday from 10 AM to 6 PM. Sometimes a company would buy the tickets so their employees could ride and play the midway games "for free." We would sell the tickets to the company for eight cents each. Rides and stands that normally charged ten to fifteen cents took one eight-cent ticket. Those that charged twenty to twenty-five cents took two eight cent tickets.

Besides picnics, there were other events for the visitors to enjoy at Crystal Beach. A home and flower show was held in the ballroom. On August 22, 1950, the American Legion Post no. 397 of Vermilion put on a well-attended boxing show in the ballroom. It was an eight bout card and the first boxing in the park since the days when Johnny Kilbane trained on the grounds. On May 26, 1951, a local dance was held by the Vermilion Veterans to raise funds for the memorial monument in Exchange Park. In 1951 a rodeo was sponsored by the

Milan Riding and Driving Club. The rodeo featured trick and fancy riding, roping steers, bronco riding, and whip cracking. There were many political ox roasts. Some had national figures in attendance such as vice-presidential candidate Henry Cabot Lodge, Governor Mike DiSalle, and Governor Frank Lausche.

If you wanted a snack, there were plenty of places throughout the park that you could visit. The popcorn stand had been popular since the beginning days of Crystal Beach. Marlene and Sandra are shown with Thelma Majorick in the late 1940s.

Here are Thelma Malcomson, and Jack and Thelma Majorick.

This food stand later became the Gillis concession for waffles, snow cones, and the most delicious french fries.

Betty and Bill Gillis also had stands on the midway.

Pete Rose and his wife ran the taffy stand. Sandra remembers watching the taffy being pulled on the machine and marveling at how the cotton candy seemed to just magically appear in the huge metal bowl. In front of the stand in this picture are Sandra, Judy Murphy, and Mary Ann Shuman, who were constant companions throughout many summers, and remain good friends today.

This was an earlier restaurant at the west entrance to the park, run by Mabel Ruby. It was in front of the rockets.

This is an aerial view of the restaurant, as well as the ballroom, rockets, caterpillar, and Nakomis.

The Dari-Delite replaced the restaurant at the west entrance. It was run by the Swope family: Bob, Eloise, and their three daughters, Gloria, Janice, and Georgia. They came from Savannah, Ohio, near Ashland, and had a cottage in Nakomis that they lived in each summer. The restaurant was later managed by the Heberling family.

Just north of the Dari-Delite and next to the Dodgem was Jungle Larry's Safari. Larry Tetzlaff use to appear at schools with his animal program. He would go to Florida in the winter and put on shows there with his animals. While performing at the park in the late 1950s, he lived with his wife and son at Elberta Beach. He would bring the lion cub in his car to the park every day along with the other animals that he kept at his home. Once he brought the lion cub to the office and signed his contract with the cub's paw.

The Sunset Years

Crystal Beach Park was a family-owned park for its entire existence. Relatives of not only the owners, but also of many who worked at the park, would come and spend their summers at Crystal Beach. Most everyone connected with the park either started with it in its infancy, or carried on where their parents left off. Many employees and their families were from Vermilion, Vermilion-on-the-Lake, Lorain, Huron, and other surrounding communities. There were also those who came from other states.

The biggest worry since the opening of the park and throughout the fifty-five seasons that it was open was always the weather. This concern was in the thoughts of everyone connected with the operation of the park. There would be a serious financial setback if it rained on a Saturday or Sunday, on a day a picnic was scheduled, on the date a big band was booked, or on any of the holidays during the summer. There were no season tickets in those days. Any income lost from rained-out days could never be made up.

Times were beginning to change in the late fifties. With these changes came different kinds of concerns. Family-owned parks were finding it more and more difficult to compete with the parks that were now becoming owned by corporations. Corporations were in a much better financial position to handle the enormous outlay of capital necessary for purchasing new and exciting rides and attractions. These yearly purchases seemed to be becoming increasingly more necessary to stimulate the public's interest.

Other factors were developing that affected Crystal Beach's ability to survive. Companies were giving up their picnics for other wage incentives. Large industrial plants were locating in Lorain, causing Vermilion-on-the-Lake to change from a vacation area of summer homes to an area of permanent residences. Other nearby vacation areas soon began to follow. Without the constant turnover of vacationers to visit the park, the attendance started to decrease. Big bands were decreas-

These two aerial views of the park show the property before and after the shopping center and motel were built.

ing in popularity, and bands were not doing as much touring around the country. Superhighways were diverting traffic that previously had passed by the park.

The beginning of the end of Crystal Beach was on August 19, 1959, when a supplemental agreement was signed between Thelma Calvert, Eleanor Ryan, Kenneth Evenson, and Walter Evenson. It was for the sale of the twenty acres south of Lake Road. The agreement stipulated that Crystal Beach could still retain the right to use a portion of the land as a parking area. This agreement remained in effect through the name change to South Shores, Incorporated, in September 1961. Kenneth and Walter Evenson remained the builders and developers of the South Shore Shopping Center. A portion of the land on the eastern side of the twenty acres was sold to Mike and Elizabeth Rusine. Mike Rusine was a Lorain businessman who constructed a motel on the property.

On November 6, 1962, the park was sold to the Vermilion Crystal Development Corporation. Originally, part of the plans for the development of Crystal Shores was for building a retirement home on the site of the park. After the death of James Fisher of Vermilion, who was the corporation's president, the officers of the Crystal Development Corporation made the decision to sell to the Bay Colony Development Corporation of Cleveland. Along with the former Crystal Beach property, the Bay Colony Development Corporation also purchased the acreage north of East Liberty Avenue and east to Elberta Beach. Agents for the sale were G. B. Kimmick of Vermilion, Lory Lazarony of Sandusky, and the Lawyers Title Insurance Company of Sandusky.

All rides and buildings were dismantled and sold except the ballroom, which remained as a roller-skating rink run by Lee and Jean Axx, and the Dari-Delite restaurant.

A public auction was held on November 17, 1962. The auctioneer was James Wagner of Amherst. The two hundred thousand board feet of lumber that had been the Thriller was sold to Francis Dean of Vermilion. Other properties that were auctioned were the shooting gallery, the fun house, and the concession stands. The Tilt-A-Whirl went to a firm in Detroit; the Tumble Bug was sold to Geauga Lake Park; and the miniature three-coach train went to Chippewa Lake.

Will and Kenneth Klingshirn, a brother partnership, acquired the property from the Bay Colony Corporation in March 1965. Their plans for developing Crystal Shores matched those begun by the former owners, which included housing and apartments.

The final event held on the grounds of Crystal Beach was Operation Open Heart's Memory Lane Ball. It was held on Saturday, October 16, 1965. Bizgrove's fifteen-piece band played for over one thousand people. They came from Vermilion, Huron, Wellington, Oberlin, Cleveland, Lorain, Huron, Amherst, and other surrounding areas to once again dance under the crystal ball. The event was held to raise money for a children's scholarship fund. The Klingshirn Builders donated the use of the ballroom. It was the last chance to dance to the big band sounds in the ballroom that had hosted many a big name band since 1925. The ballroom that had weathered the Depression, the change in musical tastes, and the conversion into a roller-skating rink was now facing the end of an era. On this night, when the lights went out and the dancing stopped, so too would the heart of what once was Crystal Beach Park.

The demolition of the ballroom was a sad sight.

When driving into Vermilion along Lake Road, now called East Liberty, it is hard to picture where the park used to be. A bank stands where the ballroom was located.

This gas station occupies the space where the Blanchat home once stood.

The white pylon, which used to have the "sweeps" or arms of the Tumble Bug attached to it, is the only physical reminder that remains of what once was Crystal Beach. Apartments stand where the arcade once stood along the lakefront.

The shopping center covers most of the land that was the parking lot.

This gentle sloping area of land shows where the hollow used to be. Those of us who grew up at Crystal Beach see a different picture than you see. We see the spot where it all began.

After 1965, Crystal Beach Park became just a memory. But for those of us who lived it…oh my, what a wonderful memory it is.

Epilogue

The memories linger on—with a little help from our friends.

As years passed, there was a growing interest in the historical places in Vermilion. The Friends of Harbortown asked Eleanor Ryan to speak in July 1993 at the old schoolhouse on Route 60 where she and her sister, Thelma had both been students. She presented a slide show on the history of Crystal Beach Park. Following the program, the audience was asked to stand if they had ever worked at the park. There were at least eighty people in attendance, and about a fourth of them stood up. It was most heartwarming to see the number of people who were proud of their connection with Crystal Beach Park. This began the idea of putting the memories from the slide show with more memories and pictures from other sources into a book.

This picture shows Jimmy Ryan, Marlene Calvert Feldkamp, Sandra Calvert Mueller, Tom Ryan, and Eleanor Ryan (seated) gathered together after the slide show.

One of the few, but major, artifacts left of the park is the beautiful crystal ball that glittered magically in the Crystal Beach Ballroom. It had been saved from destruction by the Klingshirn Builders in 1965 when the ballroom was demolished. It was first owned by the Vermilion Boat Club. They used it in their dance hall until the club was remodeled in 1993. Following the removal of the crystal ball from the boat club it was given to Tom Ryan. The historical significance and value of the crystal ball was recognized. Gene Sofranko of Lorain Glass volunteered to restore the 1,015 small mirrors and repair it to its former beauty. On Wednesday, May 31, 1995, the Lorain Lions Club presented the Guy Lombardo Orchestra at the Lorain Palace Civic Center. At 7:30 PM, the crystal ball of Crystal Beach Park was once again sending its reflected light throughout the darkened room thanks to the generosity of Tom and Carole Ryan. They had donated the crystal ball to the Civic Center in memory of his parents, Eleanor and Jimmy Ryan, and to all who had played a part in keeping the crystal ball in existence. The crystal ball continues to shine its light on theatrical performances that are held at the Lorain Palace Civic Center. Interestingly enough, members of the fifth generation of the Blanchat family have been part of some of the casts of performers.

Though memorabilia from Crystal Beach is rare, here are some mementoes from the Blanchat grandchildren's collection:

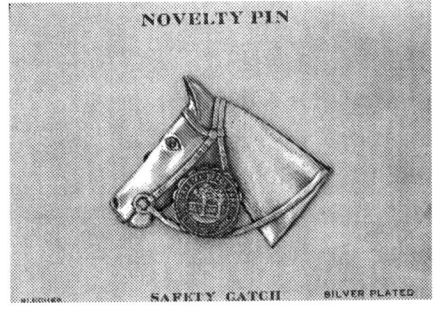

Decal

Novelty pin

Pennant

Ink blotter

This original stationary shows the addition of an insert of Marlene and Tom from a news article regarding the donation of the Crystal Beach crystal ball to the Lorain Palace Civic Center.

This is a Crystal Beach car tag.

A more recent memento of Crystal Beach Park is the wooden replica of the Crystal Beach Ballroom. Rusty Pearce of the former Harbortown Emporium in Vermilion contacted Marlene Calvert Feldkamp in regards to the creation of this item. Permission was given for the Cat's Meow Company to make these replicas in 1996.

The latest memento of the park was received from Ryan Angney, son of teacher Monica Angney and the late mayor of Vermilion Alex Angney. It was authenticated by the Great Lakes Museum in Vermilion as a part of the early square wooden pier just off the shore at Crystal Beach.

Crystal Beach Park was again remembered on Wednesday, August 9, 2000, at the Ritter Public Library in Vermilion when Marlene and Sandra provided a slide show presentation. The response from the community was overwhelming. The meeting room in the library was filled to capacity twenty minutes before the program was to begin. People stood around the walls of the room. Others were waiting outside in the library, unable to get in. The librarian announced that because of the amount of people, a second program would be given the following week. She jokingly asked that anyone who was there that night not come back next week.

The second program was held the following week, August 17th. The location was changed to the Vermilion High School auditorium.

The attendance was around 175 people. Everyone who came this time was able to find a seat.

When the program at the Ritter Library was concluded, the audience was asked to share some of their memories of the park. These responses show that when memories are made, they are not easily forgotten. They only needed a few pictures to bring them back into focus.

Eileen Popovich of Vermilion remembered the boxer Johnny Kilbane, who boxed at the ballroom, but trained east of Vermilion.

Kathy White of Sheffield Lake remembered coming to hear Jimmy Dulio's Band play when her dad, Dick Reed, was their drummer.

Gerry (Ontal) Lohman of Monroeville remembered living at the park in the cottage for a few years in the forties. Her parents worked in the park.

Rich and Jan Orseno of Amherst remembered that they spent their first date in 1952 dancing in the ballroom to Ray Anthony's Band. There were lots of great memories!

Dennis Smith of Brownhelm remembered spending many hours at the park. He remembered his mother, Marie Smith, working as a waitress in the ballroom.

Kathy and Charlie Schroeder of Vermilion remembered having lots of childhood memories and spending lots of time at the park as they were growing up. Their daughter wrote a great paper on the park.

Joe Villa of Lorain remembered working in the ballroom and all the name bands that came to play for the dances.

Paul and Corinne Cook of Lorain remembered the big bands. They had their honeymoon in one of the cottages in 1945.

Pat Smith of Vermilion remembered spending lots of time at the park with her sister because their mom and dad, Roy and Thelma Malcomson, owned and operated the penny arcade.

John and Jan Tuttle of Vermilion remembered having lots of dates going to the park.

Mike Minich of Elberta Beach, Vermilion, remembered the fireworks!

Martha Minich remembered the fireworks too, and she loved skating at the old roller rink.

Jim and Barb Wight of Wellington remembered spending summers at the park. Jim recalled at age twelve helping at the penny arcade and playing golf on the miniature golf course. Jim also remembered coming out in the summers to stay in Nakomis with his family and spending time with Tom and Marlene as well as the other kids who worked in the park. "It was a great time in my life and I will always cherish my memories," he said. An added thrill was getting the chance to play Louis Armstrong's trumpet during the band's practice session.

Alton Herman of Birmingham remembered when he took tickets in the dance hall.

Pat, John, and Dale Reising of Vermilion remembered spending many hours at the park when they were young, and have fond memories.

Katy Reutener of Vermilion remembered spending many days at the park as a little girl riding all the rides. She grew up there.

Marcus "Charles" Dubius of Vermilion remembered that his grandfather, Charlie Zoro, operated the skeeball alleys in the penny arcade.

Winifred Schaeffer of Lorain remembered "the good old days at Crystal Beach Park."

Crystal Diaz of Amherst met her husband in 1945 at one of the dances at the ballroom.

Carolyn Jones of Vermilion remembered the fun of taking the children and enjoying many evenings at the park.

B. J. Nesbitt of Amherst loved the music and wrote a book called Big Bands on the Lakefront.

Dave and Sandy Rosso of Lorain loved riding the "Duck."

Carol Murphy of Lorain remembered growing up at the park and loved riding the roller coaster and the "Bug."

Walter and Tracey Taylor of Florida worked at the park, and they loved dancing on their days off.

Marlene Young of Vermilion, who married Paul Young, remembered working at the ticket booths. She also use to ride the rides with her friend Sandy Calvert.

Maxine Hayes Schmitz of Vermilion had many memories, but the one special one was when her husband proposed to her as they sat on the benches overlooking the lake behind the penny arcade. It was during the intermission of one of the dances when they were held upstairs.

Joe and Dee Trifiletti of Lorain remembered spending lots of time dancing to the name bands on both Friday and Saturday nights.

Kathy Summers of Lorain remembered riding the silver airplanes and the "Bug." She remembered meeting Senator Henry Cabot Lodge at the ballroom in 1960. She also had her senior prom at the ballroom.

Gerald and Doris Stwan of Vermilion spent many years dancing at the ballroom. Doris worked for Jungle Larry as a clown.

Tom Judge of Vermilion worked at Crystal Beach for ten years.

Neil and Betty Meyers of Lorain remembered coming to the park every year for the picnic with U.S. Automatic of Amherst, Ohio.

Bernie Wagner of Amherst remembered that, in the early forties, *The Lorain Journal* printed coupons for five cents. Her aunt saved them and, as a surprise, took the three of them to a wonderful day at the park.

"Nuggie" Cook of Vermilion remembered dancing the marathon dances in 1932 in the ballroom above the arcade. "Danced my life away on Friday and Saturday nights," she said.

Sue Roth Opperman of Vermilion remembered at the early age of thirteen going with her art class and teacher, Marilyn Rundle, to paint various sites at the park. She recently found her painting of the frog from the merry-go-round. She is now an art teacher in the Wellington schools.

Cindy Roth Weeks recalled when her sister Sue would take her to the park to ride on the kiddie rides.

Cindy and Sue, with their brothers, Dan and Jim Roth, are the children of George and his wife, Judy Burley of Vermilion. George and his brother, Bob Roth, were the former owners of Roth Manufacturing, which had previously been White-Roth Manufacturing, a company that brought its picnics to the park.

Darlene Stinson remembered her grandfather, Gordon Sprigg, taking the whole family to the Ohio Edison Picnic at the park. Her father, Bob Sprigg, helped tighten the bolts on the roller coaster around 1938.

Bob Kyle of Vermilion remembered that his dad pulled out the parked cars that got stuck in the mud on those rainy nights in the spring.

Darlene Villa of Vermilion remembered working at the park with her dad, Joe, and her uncle, George.

Sue Backus of Vermilion remembered going to her first big dance ever on Easter Sunday in 1945 to see Tommy Dorsey.

Buddy and Leslie Ennis of Vermilion remembered lots of Sunday evenings dancing to the sounds of wonderful big bands.

Carol Orticari of Sandusky remembered when she and her sister were too young to go into the ballroom to dance. They would stand by the railing around the ballroom and listen to the great music and watch the dancers. We didn't realize at the time how lucky we were to be listening to them. Another memory was when my sister and husband would often have friends over and we would pack up hot dogs and marshmallows, cross the street, walk through the park, and go down to the beach for a cookout.

The daughter of T. J. Hume was at the Crystal Beach program. Her father built the new casino.

"Tootie" Tomes (Mary Louise Reisinger) of Vermilion remembered working at the bubble stand. She was a friend of Pete, Minnie, and Gloria Derby. She said she enjoyed skating at the rink.

Barry Lima of Vermilion remembered always dreaming of working at Crystal Beach Park, but when he was old enough, the park had closed.

The sketch of the Crystal Beach Ballroom on the following page was done for the cover of the memory book by the Blanchats' great-granddaughter, Susanne Mueller. The book was at the slide show presentation held at the Vermilion library in August 2000.

On Sunday, June 9, 2002, Marlene Calvert Feldkamp and Tom Ryan presented a program at the Museum of Carousel Art and History in Sandusky, Ohio. They had been asked to speak by Vickie Vandenbout, daughter of Joe Mayer from Vermilion. Joe Mayer is a retired Vermilion policeman who also worked at the picnics and dances at Crystal Beach.

In July 2002, Burton Nesbitt wrote the book *Big Bands on the*

Crystal Beach Park

Vermilion, Ohio

Lakefront. In the foreword, he explained how the book came to be written. He had seen an article in 1995 in the newspaper about the Crystal Beach Ballroom. This had inspired the idea to write about the dance halls along the local shores of Lake Erie. The book is a comprehensive collection of the appearances of bands listed by the year and day. Names of vocalists, band theme songs, and other information are also included.

We Blanchat grandchildren continue to perpetuate the memory of Crystal Beach Park by giving programs to historical groups, churches, schools, and other organizations. George and Josephine's great-great grandchildren Joshua, Nicholas, Michael, William, Matthew, Patrick, Olivia, Cameron, Ryan, Kelly, Nora, Claire, Emily,

Sara, and Andrew, we're sure, would have enjoyed the park as much as their grandparents.

One Fourth of July weekend, Ron Heitman brought his rocket ship car to Marlene and David Feldkamp's home. For a brief time, we were able to share a part of our past with our children and grandchildren. As we enjoyed the wind blowing on our faces and the calliope music playing, we closed our eyes and were once again at Crystal Beach.

We hope that you had a pleasant ride with us down memory lane.

Remembering Crystal Beach Park

Remember the Thriller at Crystal Beach Park?
Remember the Bug and Laff-In-The-Dark?
You and your friends, oh how you screamed!
And the laughter forever, that all of you dreamed.

You'd go to the Penny Arcade for some fun.
Then on to the rink to watch skaters till down went the sun.
Night time brought dancers to the ballroom's smooth floor
To dance to the great bands, who are now no more.

The taffy, popcorn, hot dogs and more,
The picnics and swimming off Lake Erie Shore,
Oh, how you loved to catch merry-go-round rings,
Or see just how high you could go in the swings.

For good clean fun and to watch fireworks soar,
Oh, to return to that park, just once more!

Eleanor Blanchat Ryan
1990

Printed in the United States
93804LV00004B/13-15/A